For You and For Me

by

Fathima Arshard

Contents

Hope, Positivity and Strength

Dear reader,

keep going.
Sometimes it will feel like you are stuck in a maze,
but I promise there will be an end to these tiring days.

Go past the dreaded nights that you fear,
where your thoughts are all that you can hear.

Keep going.
In time you will see,
that this isn't how it will always be.

-F.A

In chaos
you learn about yourself the most,
how strong you truly are
when being strong becomes your only choice.

-F.A

Hard days
are part and parcel of life.
If things were perfect all the time,
there would be no goals,
there would be no drive.
To win you must fight.
To succeed you must strive.
Hard days are needed to make us feel alive.

-F.A

Like a butterfly be soft,
but strong enough to soar across the sky.

-F.A

Struggles in life are like bricks.
With each one, your foundation is built.
The harder the struggle, the heavier the brick,
the stronger the cement that goes around it.
With each struggle, the stronger you become,
the harder it is for a breakdown.

-F.A

Beautiful is the flower
that is slightly torn,
from giving to others
petals of its own.

-F.A

When life unexpectedly pushes you back a step,
you are in the best position to stop and check,
and look at your future from a better view,
this time, with more experience too.
Go about things differently.
Realign your priorities.
Look at it as a sign.
Look at it as a lifeline.

-F.A

Surf above the waves of every hardship,
a chance to rise, a chance to fly,
if you put your mind to it.

-F.A

What once was a caterpillar
now flutters its precious wings in the sky,
butterflies are a reminder
that change can take you from low to high.

-F.A

You must break to build,
you must hurt to heal,
there is good in every
discomfort you feel.

-F.A

You will end up
exactly where you are meant to be,
just like every star
in the night sky that you see,
perfectly placed
surrounded by peace and serenity.

-F.A

When you are
unsure about something,
give it time.
Time makes everything clear.
Just as fog clears with time,
so will your clouded mind.

-F.A

In the jigsaw of life,
there is no such thing
as wrong pieces,
the good and the bad
are equally needed,
for the bigger picture
to be completed.

-F.A

If the sun can shine through rain,
you can smile through pain
and create rainbows
in your life again.

-F.A

Like the tightening of loose laces,
every difficulty pulls you together
to prevent you from tripping up later.

-F.A

All things are beautified
with an essence of compromise,
for even clouds must make way
so that the sun can rise.

-F.A

Beautiful things
will come your way,
if you stop rewinding
and just press play.

-F.A

Do not overthink it,
the best things happen
when you least expect it.

-F.A

Aspirations
are stepping stones,
the more you have,
the further you go,
the further you grow.

-F.A

Happiness is a mirror,
walk towards it with a smile
and it will come towards you with a smile.

-F.A

How many times
must you witness
night turn into day,
to realise that
light will always find its way.

-F.A

Even if it seems impossible
continue to try.
The number of times you fall
before you fly,
will not even matter
when you're up above,
soaring across the sky.

-F.A

Even the tallest tree
was beneath the ground one day.
Even the highest mountain
was just rocky land one day.
Even the king of the jungle
was a small cub one day.
Believe,
and it will happen someday.

-F.A

There will come a day
when tears no longer
soak your pillows at night,

when grey clouds become white
and your days are full of light.

It will take you by surprise.
Things will start to feel right.

There will come a day when
everything you have been praying for
lands right in front of your eyes.

-F.A

Be like the peacock,
delightfully strange,
whilst others rush inside
it dances in the rain.

-F.A

Let them think they've won,
as they cut off your leaves,
as they break off your stem,
as they scrunch your petals,
because what they don't know
is that your faith is the seed,
the only thing you need to succeed,
rooted deep within,
beneath the soil,
and you will blossom again,
more beautiful than ever before.

-F.A

What you give
is what you receive,
be a breath of fresh air
that someone else needs.

-F.A

Be like the sun,
clouds may surround you
but continue to shine.

-F.A

The moon is proof
that even on the darkest of nights,
if you search for it,
there will be some form of light.

Rainbows are proof
that even on the dullest of days,
if you search for it,
colours can appear so bright.

So whatever it is
that you are searching for,
don't stop until it comes to sight.

-F.A

For all the good
that you have done,
your time will come.

-F.A

Wilted roses
are still beautiful,
darling with age
your beauty is still visible.

-F.A

Heartbreak and Hardship

The worst kind of goodbye
is the one that is never said.

-F.A

They say in the world,
there are six other people
who look just like you,
well this must be true,
because this cannot be you.

Your arms
around another woman,
doing all the things
you said you wouldn't.

Blindsided
by lies every day,
all the warning signs
I pushed away.

My stomach
in knots,
my head
spinning,
the moment I realised,
it was all a lie
that I was living.

-F.A

Broken doesn't mean "the end".
Those strong enough to pick themselves up
are just beginning.

-F.A

The pain resides
yet her eyes refuse to water,
she continues to love with all her heart,
just like the queen who raised her.

-F.A

Forgiveness
is a crown
for those
who have been wronged,
gems of honour,
diamonds of dignity,
embellished without
a single penny,
allowing one to let go
to live,
rightfully worn
by those who forgive.

-F.A

…and in the end,
I thank you
for the scars you left me with,
because every time I feel them,
I pray to be kinder,
gentler, and wiser.
Your bitter acts
have only made me sweeter.

-F.A

Broken hearts
are beautiful too,
for between the cracks
run rivers that glisten,
reflecting light
from the brightest of souls.

-F.A

As I carved goodness into you,
I destroyed the monster
that you grew into.
You finally became
what I knew you could be,
hand worked perfection of mine,
but for someone else to keep.

-F.A

Boxed away
sits her heart,
a precious antique,
an exquisite one-off piece,
placed in the wrong boutique.

-F.A

Hand me the truth,
even if it pricks me
with its sharp edges,
I'd rather bleed
than be blinded by lies
you cover with smudges.

-F.A

Nails of steel
I drill into the holes you left me with,
as they loosen, I tighten them
until a perfect fit,
stronger than ever a weapon I became,
because of what you did.

-F.A

Despite the dust,
the mud, the dirt,
a rose continues to grow,
in the same way,
despite the struggle,
the trial, the hurt,
you will continue to grow.

-F.A

Hardships
are far from ideal,
but the blessings that they bring
outweigh the struggles that you feel.

-F.A

Some days it rains,
but the sun will follow.
What hurts today,
will heal tomorrow.

-F.A

Sometimes
you must hit
rock bottom,
to plant seeds
from scratch
and blossom.

-F.A

It is yourself
you need an apology from,
for caring
even once true colours are shown.

-F.A

Over two hundred bones
in the human body,
yet one's actions
can completely
break us.

-F.A

Be soft be kind and be gentle,
everyone around you is healing.

Life is a spiral of trial after trial.
Healing is a continuous cycle.

As we recover from one hurdle,
we witness another ones' arrival.
So be soft be kind and be gentle.

A calamity that may seem small to you,
may be big from someone else's point of view.
So be soft be kind and be gentle.

More importantly, we all heal differently,
some do quietly, more emotionally
whilst others do physically, more explicitly,
but the bottom line is we all heal simultaneously.

You are never alone in this cycle,
nor are you alone in this spiral of trial.
Healing is universal. Healing is the key to survival.
So be soft be kind and be gentle.

-F.A

Assumptions and Conclusions

Forgive,
but don't let history repeat,
there is a difference between
being kind and being naïve.

-F.A

Memories are both
a blessing and a pain.
There are some
I want to hold onto
for the rest of my days.
There are others
I wish I could
just simply erase.

-F.A

It's ok to overlook someone's mistakes,
but it's on you to figure out whether it's a mistake
or just a part of their trait.

-Г.A

Your future self
is looking at you right now
and is telling you to do more,
love more, say more, be more,
don't waste these days being unsure,
say yes to new opportunities
that knock on your door,
the world is yours
to explore.

-F.A

Nothing is more unfortunate
than one's existence
only being valued
once it is absent.

-F.A

When you find yourself in a situation,
where you have to make an important decision,
choose the option that is better for your future,
not just what you prefer in that moment.

The people who will be around you,
the places you will go to,
the person you will become someday,
are all affected by the decisions you make today.

Immediate gratification may be tempting,
but nothing is worse than a lifetime of regretting.
Give yourself the best help
and be good to your future self.

-F.A

It's the little things
that leave you smiling.
It's the little things
that make you happy within.
It's incredible how much joy
small gestures can bring.
Often the little things in life
are much bigger than we think.

-F.A

At your worst
count your blessings
and say thank you,
at your best
don't let pride
control your attitude,
for the simple secret
of happiness
is gratitude.

-F.A

As life goes on,
one thing you learn
is exactly that.
Life goes on.

It doesn't stop
when we are unhappy,
nor does it stop
when we are pleased.

So accept the bad
and cherish the good,
for life's just a collection
of fleeting moments when understood.

-F.A

The moment
you realise your worth,
you move from invisible
to invincible.

-F.A

You don't need to be blood related
to care for someone.

You don't need to practice the same religion
to sympathise with someone.

You don't need to be of the same colour
to help someone.

You just need the basic principles
of being a human.

-F.A

You reach a whole new level
of peace and patience,
when you learn to master
the art of acceptance.

-F.A

There comes a beautiful sense
of contentment and ease,
when you draw a line between
what you want and what you need.

-F.A

If we didn't have rain
we wouldn't appreciate the sunshine.
If we didn't have bad days
we wouldn't appreciate the good ones.
A balance of everything is needed
to always be appreciative.

-F.A

As you get older,
your circle gets smaller
because time is a detox,
those who aren't good for you
will move far away from you,
losing them is not a loss.

-F.A

Manners and morals
are like petals surrounding a flower,
for without them,
one is completely unattractive.

-F.A

We are all
works in progress.
It begins as scribbles,
a rough figure, a sketch,
shades added for depth.
An outline appears,
and splash of colours,
thousands of strokes
and even more corrections,
patience is the key to perfection.
It can take days,
it can take weeks,
to reach our potential,
our prime,
our peak,
no work of art
takes the same time
to complete,
especially you,
a masterpiece.

-F.A

You are allowed
to acknowledge your worth.
You are allowed
to put yourself first.
Self-care
doesn't make you selfish.
Those who really matter
will understand this.

-F.A

Work on
what really
matters,
your mind,
your morals,
your manners.

-F.A

Don't simplify yourself,
stay complex,
it's rare to find people
with such depth.

-F.A

Invest in those dearest to you,
not in terms of zeros at the end
but in terms of the time that you spend.

-F.A

Do not worry about
those who walk away
when things get tough,
the ones worth worrying about
stay even when things get rough.

-F.A

The kind
that make things happen,
the kind
that don't just hear, they listen,
the kind
that prove their love through action,
are the kind of people
who deserve your attention.

-F.A

Be kind to your heart,
don't place your happiness
in hands that tear it apart.

-F.A

There is a difference
between someone who wants you
and someone who wants to be with you.

-F.A

As with garments,
we too have care labels.
Find someone who reads yours.

-F.A

Do not determine
your prince charming
by what he is riding
or how he is dressed,
so long as he brings
pure love and respect,
there is nothing more
that you should expect.

-F.A

Saying sorry
and being sorry
is different
when observed,
the former
is just the sound
of five letters in one word,
the latter
goes to show
that to someone
you mean the world.

-F.A

If someone
only values your worth
once you leave,
if your efforts
are only appreciated
once you leave,
if your importance
only shows
once you leave,
realise that all along
you were the moral of their story,
how to not take good people for granted.

-F.A

Notice who is there for you
and who is only there
when they need you.

-F.A

There is nothing
more tragic,
than unspoken words.
If you feel something,
let it be heard.

-F.A

An aggressive tone
is as bad as an aggressive action.
Words can hit you, push you
and cause a reaction.

-F.A

It is easy
to please the ears with words,
but the eyes demand a lot more,
searching beyond what is merely said,
actions are what they look for.

-F.A

The best
conversations
are those about
the sky, the stars,
the little things in life,
the conversations that
don't involve people
or their lives.

-F.A

You are not
the mistakes that you *made*,
you are all
the corrections that you *make*.

-F.A

If qualities
were like ingredients,
listing exactly what we contain,
would we continue to act the same?

-F.A

Hardships in life,
can make you bitter
or make you better.
Difficulties in life,
can make you weaker
or make you wiser.
Your mind-set
is the controller.

-F.A

As you show it for others,
you gain it for yourself,
that is how the concept
of respect works.

-F.A

If complicating
simple things
were a skill,
we human beings
would be known
to excel.

-F.A

Without doubt,
without question,
one of the greatest gifts
you could give to someone
is your undivided attention.

-F.A

Whilst some
fuel your energy,
others drain your energy,
choose your companions carefully.

-F.A

Often we associate insecurities
to what our eyes can see,
but is it really a flaw
if it is only skin deep?

-F.A

So many people hear you,
but how many actually listen?
The answer to that question
can be found in their actions.

-F.A

Never underestimate others,
who knows
what their potential could be,
after all,
a flower is not born a flower,
a flower is born a seed.

-F.A

Love of Every Kind

In a world full of problems,
you are my solution.

In a world full of lies,
you are my truth.

In a world full of war,
you are my peace.

Without you,
my world is incomplete.
You are exactly what I need.

-F.A

There is so much I feel
when I'm around you,
pure love and safety
being the top two.

You carry my burdens
and you share my worries,
you're the kind of hero
I only hear of in stories.

Your actions prove
that your love for me is true,
this kind of comfort
is something I only feel with you.

It's every girl's dream
to find a man just like you,
thank you for loving me
in the beautiful way that you do.

-F.A

Every memory I have with you
is one that I adore,
with each day that passes by
in awe of you I grow.

-F.A

The perfect person does not exist,
but perfect traits in a person do exist.

-F.A

My love, you are like the perfect effortless sun,
the sun that shines for absolutely everyone,

but when the day draws to an end,
and you are exhausted and need a friend,

I will be the clouds that move towards you,
the clouds you can hide into,

to protect you and keep you whole overnight,
so that you always enter the next day shining bright.

-F.A

When it's right
you won't even need to try,
the grass will look a little greener,
the sun will shine a little brighter,
the universe will come together
to show you that this one's a keeper.

-F.A

Like the first drops of rainfall
following a drought,
you are all that I've ever been
praying about.

-F.A

For me,
you are not one in a million,
you are a million in one,
for you possess a million things
that I'd want in someone.

-F.A

One day
someone will walk into your life,
brush off the dust from your bookshelf
and read every story of yours.

The chosen one,
who appreciates you,
treasures you
and opens new doors.

The one free from secrets,
free from lies
and is nothing but truthful.

Just remember,
it gets ugly
before it gets beautiful.

-F.A

If you find someone
whose values are parallel to yours,
whose morals are in sync with yours,
who you never feel the need to doubt,
who steals words right out of your mouth,
who you picture in your own reflection,

hold onto them,
they are the textbook definition
of perfection.

Opposites may attract
but to find someone so similar to you
is what soul mates are all about,
something some people go a lifetime without.

-F.A

Your arms
are the walls
I want to find shelter in,
your eyes
are the windows
I want to see the world with,
and your heart
is the room
I want to stay forever in.
I have found a home in you.

-F.A

In a book full of pages,
yours is my favourite.
The page that I fold,
the page I re-read,
the page I take out
and keep.

-F.A

Like sweet fragrance
that evaporates into air,
I feel you around
even when you are not there.

-F.A

Even the rockiest roads
and the steepest hills in life,
will feel like a walk in the park
with the right person by your side.

-F.A

…and then
someone will appear,
as if from thin air,
and they will be as perfect
as one can get,
like the morning sunrise,
and the evening sunset,
someone you'll never
grow tired of looking at.

-F.A

I feel your presence
from a distance,
everyone else is
non-existent.
You call me
without uttering a word.
Eye contact,
talking without being heard.

-F.A

Through the eyes
of the one meant for you,
all your imperfections
look perfect on you.

-F.A

One of the most
comforting things
in a world full of
uncertainty,
is knowing that
family love
comes with a
lifetime guarantee.
Despite the lows
and highs,
despite the fuss
and fights,
family love,
is the kind of love
for life.

-F.A

You ask me
"what's the biggest
luxury in this world?"

I say, it's those who
love you even at your worst.

Seven billion humans
exist on this earth,
yet they continue
to put you first.

-F.A

They are like stars
that you can wish upon,

they take your problems
as their own,

they help you with what you need
and what you want,

blessed are those who have family
who go above and beyond.

-F.A

The most
selfless person
I've ever known,
built me a house
in her heart
that I call my own,

one that is not
made of brick or stone,
but one that sheltered me
from when I was born.

Mother,
you're the person
who springs to mind
when I think of the word
"home".

-F.A

Loving,
from the second
I was born,
it comes to her
so naturally.

I cry, I fuss,
I groan and moan,
she's still there for me.

From her I take
a lifetime loan,
she still gives
endlessly.

Mother,
like you there is no other,
everyone else is secondary.

-F.A

I know a man
whose arms carried me high
on days that I felt low.
A man whose arms I'll never outgrow.

I know a man
who taught me everything in life,
through many storms he survived.
A man who is forever a hero in my eyes.

I know a man,
loving, caring, considerate.
A voice of encouragement. A pillar of strength.
A man I hold close to my heart until the end.

-F.A

For the several nights
you stayed awake,

for the countless mistakes
you forgave,

for the hundreds of tears
you wiped away,

for the thousands of things
you made and gave,

for the billions of smiles
you put on my face,

I am grateful for you, Father
every single day.

-F.A

When your tiny hands
and little arms reach out for me,
when you look at me
like I am all that you know,
as if nothing else in the world matters
if you have me,
I feel the luckiest,
because my love, a lot of the times,
I have needed you
more than you have needed me.
I may be your mother,
but you are my motivation.

-F.A

Here are a few promises
I intend to keep.

I'll stay awake,
to ensure you are asleep.

I'll face any hardship,
to ensure you are at ease.

I'll give you my love and time,
to make sure you grow up just fine.

Oh sweet baby, I hope you can see,
that I will always put you before me.

-F.A

We may be in different places,
we may be doing different things,
we may not always see each other
or speak as much as people think,

but it only takes one conversation
to feel closer than ever again,
speaking of old memories
and laughing for hours on end.

Siblings have a special gift
of always staying the same,
even when everything around us
does nothing but change.

-F.A

Auntie,
you are like magic.
One moment you are a mother to me,
you protect me like I am your own,
with all your advice I have grown.
The next moment you are my best friend,
you make me laugh, you make me smile,
you always go the extra mile.
In my heart there is a special place for you,
filled with nothing but love and gratitude.

-F.A

The heart of a home
is the people who live in it,
through the memories they make in it
and the moments they treasure in it.
Regardless of its style or size,
a home is made beautiful
by the love and warmth that it holds inside.

-F.A

Nothing
is better than
finding a sister
in your best friend,
or a best friend
in your sister.

-F.A

The best kind of people
are those who can be near
even when miles apart,
distance does not dictate
who is close to one's heart.

-F.A

The best kind of friendships
are like photos in a frame,
with time things will never change,
photos always stay the same.

-F.A

Our World

Imagine doing nothing wrong and being punished.
Imagine owning a home and seeing it demolished.

Imagine having children who have nothing to eat.
Imagine being sick and having no healthcare to seek.

Imagine fleeing, not knowing where you're headed.
Imagine constantly being attacked and targeted.

Imagine relying on foreign aid for water and clothes.
Imagine seeking shelter in abandoned places and roads.

Imagine living in the world's harshest conditions.
Imagine if it were us in these situations.

-F.A

Let the liars lie,
let the frauds fake,

let the jealous envy,
let the selfish take,

let the two-faced gossip,
let the hypocrites preach,

whilst they ruin their image
it's your integrity you keep.

-F.A

The world
gives us a chance,
it gives us a platform,

the world
is our friend,
it gives us a home.

What do we do in return?
We vandalise, we litter,
we could do so much better,
we waste and spend,
all of its rules we bend,

worst of all we drain it,
and drive it to an end.

-F.A

Sunkissed sand
and pebbles,
there is something magical
about travels.

-F.A

Beaming streaks
of red pass by,

shades of orange
meet the eye,

splashing magic
across the sky,

the sun sets
and waves goodbye.

-F.A

Isn't it true?
There is so much beauty
around you.
One look at the sky,
its beautiful shades of blue
can lift up your mood,
in ways you never knew.

-F.A

Dusty winds,
roaring thunders,
all around he sits
and wonders.

Teary eyes,
scabby knees,
not a soul checks
if he breathes.

A life with no advice,
no caution,
lived by this little boy,
an orphan.

Bound by the pavement
and the streets,
this is his daily life
on repeat.

-F.A

Left and right
they turn,
empty stomachs
churn.

Filthy water,
no showers,
walk for miles,
search for hours.

How can we compare,
to those who even in despair,
do not question why life is unfair?

-F.A

Beneath the sheltering roof,
besides the warm fireplace,
sat in the comfort of my home,
tears run down my face.

How selfish am I,
demanding my own space,
whilst those less able,
genuinely lost, unstable,
pray for someone to turn to,
reach for a hand to pull through.

Look at life from their view,
all the selfish moments
you would undo.

-F.A

I pray for this diseased world,
in innocent blood it leaks,

I pray for those losing their
mothers and fathers as we speak,
the ones who witness
their brothers and sisters
pleading on their knees,
the ones whose
sons and daughters
have been missing
for over weeks,

I pray for a stop,
for an end to their grief,

I pray that
after all the difficulty they face,
comes everlasting peace.

-F.A

Wipe away insecurities,
perfection is merely
an unhealthy standard
created by society.

-F.A

How wonderful
would the world be,
if we updated our hearts
as frequently
as we update
the latest technology?

-F.A

Imagine
using your last coin
to speak to someone
on a payphone,

imagine
handwriting a letter
and sending it to your
loved ones' home,

imagine how meaningful
your conversations would be,

Oh how I'm living
in the twenty-first century,
dreaming of
how times used to be.

-F.A

Softness
is not a weakness.
To be soft in a harsh world
is an achievement.

-F.A

Be the one
who smiles first,
who helps first,
who forgives first,
time is too precious,
life is too short
to wait around for others.

-F.A

Enticing
through every word she spoke
and when she didn't,
her manners spoke a thousand words.

Sparks,
not just from her eyes
but from the aura, all around her.

Feelings of warmth,
feelings of delight,
all wrapped up with a ribbon on.

Her beauty is of a different kind.
The kind that is not just on the surface.
For beauty only recognised by the eyes,
is worthless.

-F.A

…and just like that
she can transform,

from gentle raindrops
to the strongest storm,

a woman can do both,
a woman can do it all.

-F.A

Darling
you are not an option,
nor are you an embellishment.

You are not an add-on,
nor are you an accessory.

You do not exist
just for eyes to see.

You are an empress,
with your mind,
with your soul,
you can rule the world,
so darling
be whatever you want to be.

-F.A

Printed in Great Britain
by Amazon